DISCOVER East Anglia

John Potter

▲▲ **Holme next the Sea** The beach at Holme on the shores of the Wash is a key migration point for wild birds.

▲ **Lavenham** This pretty market town in Suffolk is famous for its pastel-coloured half-timbered buildings.

CONTENTS

MYRIAD

HISTORIC NORFOLK

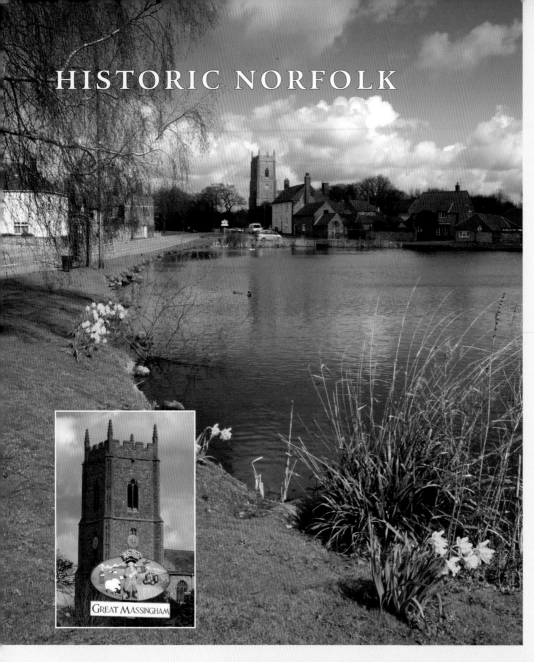

Houghton Hall, in the north-east corner of Norfolk, was the home of Robert Walpole, Britain's first prime minister.

◀ Great Massingham

A picture postcard village east of King's Lynn, Great Massingham has an enormous village green and several attractive large ponds, some of which were used as fishponds for the 11th century Augustinian abbey which once stood here. The beautiful village sign depicts Great Massingham's agricultural heritage and its former 11th century Augustinian abbey. The twin village of Little Massingham lies a few miles to the north. The great square tower of St Mary's church dominates the village skyline and houses four bells. The church has a magnificent 13th century porch. Once a year the church is used to display artefacts associated with the now disused Massingham airfield to the east of the village, a centre of bomber command during the Second World War. The Peddars Way long-distance trail which links this area with the coastal villages of north Norfolk passes to the west of Great Massingham.

▶ **Houghton Hall** This fine Palladian mansion was built by Sir Robert Walpole between 1722-1735. He was Britain's first prime minister and served in the reign of George I and George II. The architects were Colen Campbell and James Gibbs. The house was built by Thomas Ripley, and the huge and imposing stable block by William Kent. The Walpoles, a landowning family from the villages of Walpole St Peter and Walpole Cross Keys, came to the area as lords of the manor in 1307.

▶ **Walpole St Peter and Walpole St Andrew** The two Walpoles were once separate villages but they are now joined together. The famous 13th century church hosts a spectacular annual flower festival which welcomes visitors from all over the country. Close by are the superb Walpole Water Gardens boasting exotic plants, 20 different kinds of eucalyptus, palms, bananas and grasses, black swans, ornamental ducks and koi carp.

▶ **Bircham** The restored windmill in Great Bircham, a few miles north-east of King's Lynn, is a wonderful attraction for visitors. The village is set amidst gently rolling fertile farmland typical of this area of north Norfolk. At one time the region had over 300 mills grinding corn for cattle and for horse-feed and bread-making. Today very few mill buildings remain and most of those are in ruins. Dating from 1846, Bircham has been fully restored and is the only mill in the area still in working order and open to the public. Visitors can climb all five floors to the fan stage where there are superb panoramic views of the surrounding countryside. The church of St Mary the Virgin, in the centre of the village, is well known for its peal of bells.

▲ **Castle Acre** This peaceful village is known for the twin ruins of Castle Acre castle and Castle Acre priory. Founded by William the Conqueror and his wife in 1090, it rapidly developed into one of England's largest priories. Today the building lies in ruins but the prior's house and chapel still stand. The castle remains consist of huge earth banks surrounding a bailey with a motte and the remains of a keep. Castle Acre contains a large number of flint and cobble cottages centred on Stocks Green, an attractive village green planted with large lime trees and once the site of the village stocks.

ROYAL COUNTRY

The Sandringham Estate, with its beautiful grounds and unspoilt villages, lies close to Castle Rising a few miles inland from Norfolk's beautiful west coast.

▶ **Castle Rising** The keep at Castle Rising, north-east of King's Lynn, is the most spectacular remnant of the massive stone structure built by William d'Aubigny around 1150 to celebrate his marriage to the widow of Henry I and his acquisition of the earldom of Sussex. The ruins of the castle are surrounded by massive earth banks and ditches and the site is an ideal spot to view the surrounding countryside and the village.

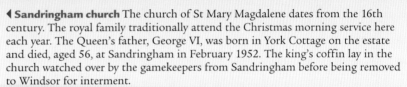

◀ **Sandringham church** The church of St Mary Magdalene dates from the 16th century. The royal family traditionally attend the Christmas morning service here each year. The Queen's father, George VI, was born in York Cottage on the estate and died, aged 56, at Sandringham in February 1952. The king's coffin lay in the church watched over by the gamekeepers from Sandringham before being removed to Windsor for interment.

▼ **West Newton** The attractive village of West Newton is part of the Sandringham estate, which also includes the villages of Wolferton, Appleton, Flitcham, Anmer and Sherbourne. Situated in an area of outstanding natural beauty close to the north Norfolk coast, the pretty village boasts a cluster of flint and rubble buildings including the primary school, which is located in the centre of the village near to the church.

◀ **Sandringham** The country retreat of the Queen and the Duke of Edinburgh, the estate has been passed down through four generations of British monarchs. Sandringham House, its museum, church and gardens are open to the public and each year thousands of visitors flock to the Sandringham Flower Show. The gardens cover 60 acres and are home to rare and historic trees, together with King George VI's garden, designed by Sir Geoffrey Jellicoe, two large lakes and a stream walk as well as Queen Alexandra's Nest, the charming summerhouse perched above the upper lake. Rhododendrons, camellias, magnolias, azaleas, hydrangeas and fuchsias all provide spectacular displays of colour. The royal family usually spend Christmas at Sandringham and remain there until February. The house and the surrounding area are much loved by the family: George V (1865-1936) wrote, "Dear old Sandringham, the place I love better than anywhere else in the world".

NORFOLK'S WEST COAST

The west coast of Norfolk faces the wide expanse of the Wash and is famous for its panoramic sunsets over the sea.

▶ **Snettisham** South of Hunstanton on the north Norfolk coast, Snettisham is a pretty village with an RSPB nature reserve two miles to the west. It looks across the Wash towards Lincolnshire and is one of the best places in Britain to see spectacular flocks of migrating birds on the move. At high tide, when the sea water covers large areas of the mudflats, thousands of wading birds take flight and move away from their feeding grounds onto the surrounding islands and mud banks. The Country Park is a popular venue for visitors with a host of attractions including a unique deer park.

▲ **Heacham** Visitors to this unspoilt family resort will enjoy uninterrupted views across the 20 mile flat landscape of the Wash. Heacham is the home of England's premier lavender farm, which is based at Caley Mill on the eastern side of the village. More than 150 varieties of lavender are cultivated here, and the farm hosts a lavender festival each July when the crop is harvested and distilled. In early summer the scent of lavender drifts in the air for miles around.

▲ **Hunstanton** "Sunny Hunny", as Hunstanton is often called, is 15 miles east of King's Lynn and has some of the best surf on the east coast of Norfolk. The town's eye-catching striped cliffs have resulted from layers of different coloured rocks being deposited over the millennia. This is a popular spot for fossil-hunters and it is not unusual at weekends to find groups armed with hammers and chisels trying to prise specimens from the cliffs.

▲ **The Old Lighthouse** Old Hunstanton, the picturesque village just east of Hunstanton, has a medieval church, two pitch and putt golf courses, a championship golf course, coastal footpaths and a nature reserve. The town's most prominent landmark is the Old Lighthouse. Beacons or lantern lights have been used to warn shipping of the dangers along this coast for centuries and the first lighthouse was built here in 1666. The present building was constructed in 1844.

NELSON COUNTRY

Horatio Nelson, Britain's greatest naval commander, was born in Burnham Thorpe. His boyhood years were spent on the creeks of the county's north coast where he got his first taste for seafaring.

▲ **Brancaster** The clubhouse of the Royal West Norfolk Golf Course dominates the beach at Brancaster. The vast stretch of sandy beach, fringed in part by beautiful sand dunes, makes this area popular for family holidays, beach-combing and birdwatching. Brancaster alone has 2,000 acres of beach and over 4.5 miles of coastline, owned by the National Trust. The area is an important breeding ground for birds and is the site of a Roman fort. Watersports are also catered for, with sailing and windsurfing lessons available at both Brancaster and Burnham Overy Staithe. It is reputed that the young Nelson first learned to sail off the coast at Brancaster.

▶▼ **The Burnhams** Burnham Market is the largest of the wonderful cluster of villages known as the Burnhams. Situated just a stone's throw from the central Norfolk coast and close to Brancaster and Wells-next-the-Sea, Burnham Market has remained unchanged for centuries. Its attractive main street is lined with a wide variety of independent specialist shops. Burnham Overy Staithe, with its challenging tidal creek waters and traditional chandlery offering boat storage and repairs, is a honeypot for boating enthusiasts. Boat trips run from here to Scolt Head during the summer season. A little further inland Burnham Thorpe is much quieter and has strong connections with the illustrious naval hero Horatio Nelson who was born here. The bust of the great commander is in the chancel of All Saints church, often known as "Nelson's church", where his father was once rector. The Lord Nelson pub in Burnham Thorpe offers a rum-based brew known as "Nelson's blood".

▶ **Tower Mill, Burnham Overy**
The majestic mill at Burnham Overy is one of only two Norfolk mills powered both by water and wind. Built in 1737 the mill lay derelict for most of the 20th century; it has recently been converted into residential accommodation. In summer the verges and hedgerows in this part of Norfolk explode with flowers and provide an excellent habitat for wildlife. Here the mill is attractively framed by the wild chicory plants which grow along the edge of the surrounding cornfields.

▲ **Holkham Hall** This beautiful 18th century Palladian-style country house was built between 1734-1762 for Thomas Coke, first Earl of Leicester. The house is set in 300 acres of magnificent landscaped parkland just west of Wells-next-the-Sea and has remained substantially unchanged since its completion. Among its highlights is the ceiling of the spectacular 50ft high Marble Hall, from a design by Inigo Jones, and the opulent salon where paintings by Rubens, Van Dyck and many others are on display. The park has its own five-mile seafront and a herd of 600 fallow deer. In 1776 the newly completed house was passed on to Thomas William Coke (1754-1842). Thomas was the MP for Norfolk for over 50 years and became famous as one of Britain's greatest-ever agricultural reformers.

THE NORTH NORFOLK HERITAGE COAST

The coastline between Holme next the Sea and Weybourne is a landscape of saltmarsh and sand dunes, interspersed with historic villages constructed from local flint. This area has some of Britain's best nature reserves.

▲ **Blakeney** In the Middle Ages this much-loved coastal village was a busy commercial port. Today the estuary has silted up and only smaller boats can weave their way through the marshes between the sand hills and mud banks. Owned by the National Trust since 1912, Blakeney Point is a 3.5 mile sand and shingle spit, which can only be reached by boat or by walking along the beach from Cley. This is a world-renowned nature reserve and bird sanctuary where record numbers of birds and wild plants can be seen. The seal colony numbers around 400.

▶ **Cley windmill** Cley next the Sea was once one of the busiest ports in Britain and the windmill stood amidst warehouses and wharves. In its early years the town had a reputation for piracy and smuggling until, in 1673, local landowner Sir Henry Calthorpe drained the marshes. The village trail takes visitors past many historic sites.

▶ **Salthouse Marshes** Seen here at dusk, the marshes are one of a string of important birding sites along the north Norfolk coast. This is an area where the sea periodically breaks through the fragile pebble banks leaving lagoons of brackish water which attract a wide variety of wading birds. As its name suggests, the village of Salthouse was once a centre for salt storage; the nearby Sarbury Hill, to the west, was an area of salt production. The village itself is a small settlement of flint and whitewashed cottages with a local pub, the Dun Cow. To the back of the village the land rises steeply; from the top of the ridge at Salthouse Heath there are extensive views of the village and its handsome church dedicated to St Nicholas, the patron saint of fishermen.

▲ **Wells-next-the-Sea** Brightly-painted beach huts nestle beneath pine woodland which fringes the long sweeping beach at Wells-next-the-Sea. Despite its name this charming resort now stands about one mile from open water. The village is packed with historic houses and narrow lanes, or "yards", which lead down to the bustling quayside. At low tide the beach seems to stretch to the far horizon and there are striking views to the west towards Holkham and Burnham Overy Staithe.

THE NORFOLK SEASIDE

The classic resorts of Cromer and Sheringham retain much of their Victorian and Edwardian charm and appeal to lovers of the traditional "bucket and spade" seaside holiday.

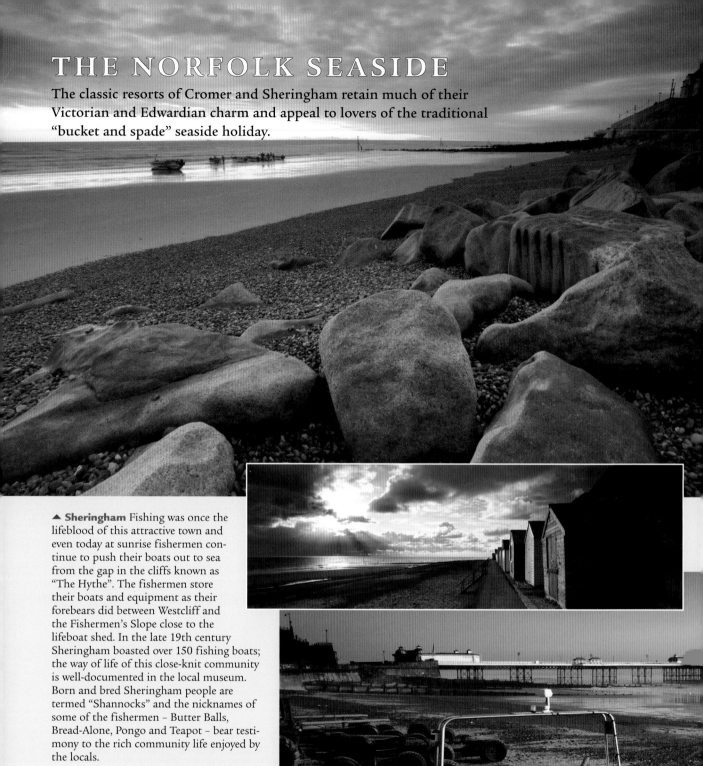

▲ **Sheringham** Fishing was once the lifeblood of this attractive town and even today at sunrise fishermen continue to push their boats out to sea from the gap in the cliffs known as "The Hythe". The fishermen store their boats and equipment as their forebears did between Westcliff and the Fishermen's Slope close to the lifeboat shed. In the late 19th century Sheringham boasted over 150 fishing boats; the way of life of this close-knit community is well-documented in the local museum. Born and bred Sheringham people are termed "Shannocks" and the nicknames of some of the fishermen – Butter Balls, Bread-Alone, Pongo and Teapot – bear testimony to the rich community life enjoyed by the locals.

▶ **Cromer** The magnificent Edwardian pier with its 510-seat Pavilion Theatre is one of the major attractions of Cromer, Norfolk's premier seaside resort. The town's expansion as a fashionable destination was hastened in the late Victorian era when a rail link from Norwich and the Midlands led to the construction of many grand hotels. The town was a firm favourite with wealthy families from Norwich who built magnificent summer homes here.

▶ West Runton This quiet village is a stop on the picturesque Bittern railway line which links Norwich with the north Norfolk coastal towns of Cromer and Sheringham. The village sits high on the top of the cliffs at Cromer Ridge, which runs from Cromer to Holt. Holidaymakers love the safe sandy beach and a favourite summer pastime is to comb the rockpools and low cliffs. A local attraction is the Shire Horse Centre which has a wonderful collection of these beautiful animals with the agricultural machinery they powered in the recent past. The village sensationally hit the headlines in 1995, when the well-preserved skeleton of a mammoth – the "West Runton Elephant" – was excavated from the cliffs. Just behind the village the National Trust has acquired an area of woodland and heath where there was once a Roman camp. At 328ft (100m) above sea level this is the highest point in Norfolk.

THE BROADS

This region of rivers and lakes lies on the border of Norfolk and Suffolk. Peat digging over millions of years has created this evocative landscape.

▲ **Hickling Broad** The largest of the navigable lakes in the Broads, Hickling Broad covers over 14,000 acres. The moorings at Hickling Broad by the Pleasure Boat Inn are a popular port of call and the secluded village of Hickling is just a stroll away. The nature reserve here is maintained by the Norfolk Wildlife Trust. These thatched boathouses were photographed early in February on a bitterly cold morning following a light frost.

◀ **Horsey Mill** This fully restored drainage windpump has been owned by the National Trust since 1948. It was entirely rebuilt in 1912, and stands proudly beside the edge of Horsey Mere between Sea Palling and Winterton-on-Sea. The redbrick building has five storeys and from the top visitors can enjoy superb views of the Broads and coast. Mills were often used as a convenient hiding place for contraband by smugglers. At times of war they have been drafted into service as lookout towers.

◀ **Blood Hill wind farm** These modern wind turbines are located to the east of Winterton-on-Sea on either side of a minor road that runs from East Somerton towards Gibbet Hill. The 10 turbines were constructed in 1992 as one of the first wind farms in Britain. They generate enough power to supply around 1,000 homes. The names Blood Hill and Gibbet Hill are a reminder of the area's violent history – a battle took place here between Saxons and Vikings reputedly so terrible that the hills ran red with blood.

▶ **How Hill** The magnificent thatched Arts & Crafts country house at How Hill is on the river Ant close to the village of Ludham. Formerly a private house, it is now a study centre surrounded by a 365-acre estate which contains the delightful Toad Hole Cottage Museum. Located in an original marshman's cottage, it gives visitors a fascinating insight into Victorian life on the Broads. There are three restored windmills at How Hill including the evocative Turf Fen windmill (right).

NORWICH

Dominated by its beautiful cathedral, the centre of the county town of Norfolk is packed with historic treasures including the unusual castle which houses the city museum.

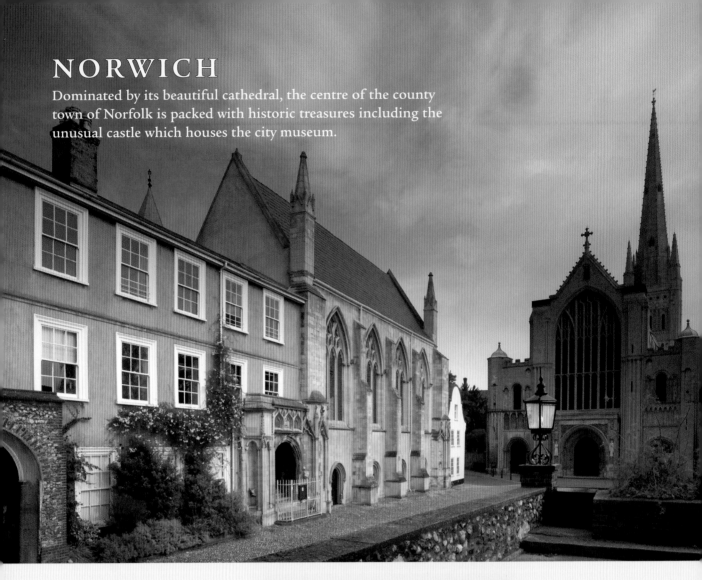

▲ Norwich Cathedral The magnificent cathedral of the Holy and Undivided Trinity looms over the city centre and is the focus of spiritual life in Norfolk. Norwich is an ecclesiastical city with over 57 medieval churches built within the city walls, 31 of which are still standing. Founded in 1096 it has the second highest spire in England which soars to 315ft (96m) and makes the cathedral the most distinctive landmark in East Anglia. The roof of the nave is embellished with over 1,000 carved bosses (far right) that depict biblical characters and scenes from the lives of the saints; this magnificent work of art is considered to be one of the finest treasures of medieval Europe. The cathedral is separated from the busy streets of the city centre by sturdy flint walls which protect the cathedral close (above) and create a tranquil oasis for city-dwellers and visitors.

◄ Cathedral cloisters
The impressive two-storey cloisters, built between 1297-1430, are second only in size to those at Salisbury cathedral. They were built to replace the original cloisters which were destroyed by fire in 1272 during riots at an annual market fair in the town. The cloisters were a key part of the original Benedictine monastery and even today there is a sense of the role the cloisters played in the monks' lives – they were the places in which the monks would read, write and teach. Doors from the cloisters led to the chapter house, the dormitory stairs, the infirmary, library, refectory and the "locutory", where the monks would talk to visitors. This now houses the cathedral shop.

▲ **Norwich Castle** The castle at Norwich was originally a wooden motte and bailey construction built by William the Conqueror in 1067 to serve as his royal palace in eastern England; by the later Middle Ages it was being used as a prison. All that exists now is the central keep which was clad in Bath stone by the architect Anthony Salvin between 1835-8. Today the keep is the entrance to the city museum which has many child-friendly interactive displays of East Anglian life, from Boudicca to the Anglo-Saxons and Vikings. The art gallery has a fine collection of porcelain and modern British paintings, especially landscapes of East Anglia.

CAMBRIDGE

Glorious architecture, green
meadows and the sight of punts
on the river Cam give Cambridge
a romantic air that is almost
unique among British cities.

▲ **The university** The second oldest university in the
English-speaking world, the
university of Cambridge was
founded in 1200. King's
College (above) dates from
1441. It is a superb example
of Gothic architecture and
its famous chapel is home to
the renowned King's College
choir, whose Christmas Eve
service is broadcast around
the world. The Baron of Beef
in Bridge Street is one of the
city's famous historic pubs.

◄ Market Hill The city's busy market takes place in front of the University Church; commonly known as Great St Mary it dominates Market Hill. A climb up the tower is a highlight of a visit to the city. There has been a church on this site since the early 13th century and the building was used for annual ceremonies, such as the conferment of degrees, until the Senate House was built in 1730.

▼ College gardens The gardens of Clare College, the second oldest Cambridge college, form part of the famous Backs – the rear part of many of the colleges which border the river. These beautiful gardens are sited on ancient fenland and contain many rare plants.

◄ Punting No visit to the city is complete without a trip in a punt along the river Cam. These traditional flat-bottomed boats were once widely used in the Fens.

▶ Grantchester Two miles upstream from Cambridge is the beautiful village of Grantchester. It is famous for its water meadows, the Orchard Tea Gardens and the Old Vicarage (right) home of the poet Rupert Brooke; his statue stands in the driveway.

ELY, THE CATHEDRAL CITY

The city of Ely is an elegant regional centre dominated by its cathedral which is known locally as the "ship of the Fens".

▶ **Ely Cathedral** Completed in 1189, the cathedral is a remarkable example of Romanesque architecture; "the Octagon", an eight-sided tower in the centre of the church (right), is the only Gothic dome in existence. The cathedral is set within the walls of a Benedictine monastery and is famous for its choir and organ music. The south transept of the cathedral houses the Stained Glass Museum. This magnificent collection has exhibits from 1,300 years of British glass manufacture and includes works by Raphael, William Morris and John Piper. In the shadow of the cathedral is Oliver Cromwell's house, where he and his family moved in 1636. The house now houses an Oliver Cromwell museum with many artefacts from the life of the family.

▼ The Quayside Until the draining of the Fens in the 17th century, Ely was an island. It is now situated on the Great Ouse and, until the 18th century, was a significant port until the arrival of the railways. In 1944, when the country was still in the grip of war, the university boat race between Oxford and Cambridge took place in Ely – the only time the race has been contested away from the Thames in its 150 year history. The town is still popular with boating enthusiasts and has a large marina; visitors can take a trip along the river in a narrow-boat to Cambridge. The Quayside has been beautifully restored with inns and restaurants. The Maltings has been redeveloped from a brewery which dates from 1868. The picturesque Prickwillow Engine House is located on the river Lark to the north-east of the city.

THE NORTH SUFFOLK COAST

Charming holiday resorts and pretty inland towns characterise the beautiful coastline of north Suffolk.

▲ **Southwold** This elegant seaside town has an atmosphere and charm that is quintessentially English. Bounded by the North Sea to the east, the river Blyth and Southwold harbour to the south-west, and Buss Creek to the north, Southwold is virtually an island. The surrounding countryside is picturesque with many pretty villages. The river Blyth estuary with its reedbeds and saltings, woodlands, open heaths and gently rolling farmland is popular for boating. Fishing was the town's main industry for over 900 years, with herring being particularly important. In the past catches were so good that there was a tithe levied on fish paid to the local parish. The town's history is preserved at the Sailor's Reading Room, one of four splendid museums in Southwold. At the western end of the high street, beyond St Bartholomew's Green, is the vast edifice of St Edmund's (middle right), which dates from the 15th century.

▶ **Dunwich** Once the capital of East Anglia, Dunwich was a major trading, fishing and ship-building centre. But coastal erosion took its toll and much of the town was lost to the sea. Dunwich once had eight churches and almost all had to be abandoned. Today the village lies between the heath to the north and Minsmere nature reserve to the south.

▼ **Walberswick** Just across the river Blyth from Southwold, Walberswick was once a thriving port. Today the village is a popular destination with an attractive harbour and a village green surrounded by quaint houses. It is famous for hosting the British Open Crabbing Championships each year.

◀ **Blythburgh** This captivating small village in north-east Suffolk, a few miles west of Southwold, lies close to the banks of Blyth Water, a tidal lagoon. The stunning medieval church of Holy Trinity, known as "the Cathedral of the Marshes", dominates the river estuary and is a beacon for local sailors.

▶ **Framlingham Castle** This magnificent building has 13 towers linked by a curtain wall and beautiful views of the reed-fringed mere, surrounding countryside and town can be enjoyed from the battlements. It was at Framlingham that Mary Tudor was proclaimed Queen following the death of her father Henry VIII.

THE SUFFOLK HERITAGE COAST

Along this unique coast shingle beaches and spits of land which reach out into the sea are interspersed with marshes and reedbeds.

▶▼ **Aldeburgh** This charming fishing village has a long and steeply shelved shingle beach, dotted with working boats and fishing huts where you can buy fresh fish. The town has always attracted painters and photographers and was the home of the composer Benjamin Britten, one of whose operas, *Peter Grimes*, is set in the Aldeburgh fishing community. A stunning memorial to the composer in the shape of two giant scallop shells, designed by artist Maggi Hambling, sits on the beach where Britten took his daily walks. Also on the beach are two lifeboat stations. One is a large modern building and the other was formerly used as a lookout station. The town's 16th century brick and timber Moot Hall is still in use today as the office of the town clerk and as a museum.

Orford Situated between Orford Ness, Tunstall Forest and Rendlesham Forest, Orford is an unspoilt fishing and tourist village south of Aldeburgh. Its cluster of narrow streets and quaint fishermen's cottages running up from the quay appear to have been little affected by the 21st century. Originally the settlement developed around the 12th century royal castle, and today the 90ft (27m) keep dominates the small town and its surroundings. The town was both politically and commercially important during the reign of Henry II, who built the castle between 1165 and 1173 to defend the area against seaborne invaders. Today, visitors come to the area to visit the keep and enjoy views across the estuary from the top of the battlements, to explore Havergate Island Bird Sanctuary or to walk the large shingle spit of Orford Ness.

Snape Maltings A unique cluster of 19th century malthouses and granaries nestles beside the river Alde five miles inland from Aldeburgh. The site houses the famous concert hall which hosts the annual Aldeburgh Music Festival. Other old buildings in the complex are now galleries, shops and restaurants. A tragic fire destroyed the first concert hall in 1969 but it was rebuilt in time for the following year's festival. In 1979, the adjacent barley store was converted into the Britten-Pears School, commemorating composer Benjamin Bitten and his partner the singer Peter Pears. The nearby quay, built to accommodate barges bringing coal to the maltings and carrying malt to breweries, is now lined with pleasurecraft and ferry boats.

St John the Baptist This beautiful church stands on high ground approximately one mile north of the village of Snape and a short walk from the Maltings. The nave was built in the 13th century and the tower and porch added in the 15th century.

SOUTH SUFFOLK

A combination of historic market towns and the busy port of Felixstowe add interest to this corner of the county.

▲▼▶ **Lavenham** A few miles north-east of Sudbury, this beautiful village is famous for its collection of half-timbered buildings, many painted in pastel colours. Lavenham was one of the richest towns in Britain during the late Middle Ages thanks to the prosperity of the local wool trade. The Guildhall of Corpus Christi (below) overlooks the market square and was established in 1592 by one of three wool guilds set up to regulate the industry. The lavish church of St Peter and St Paul (right), which stands like a sentinel on a hilltop at one end of the high street, was rebuilt in the 15th century to celebrate the Tudor victory at Bosworth Field. It has a 141ft (43m) tower – the tallest village church tower in Britain.

▶▲ **Felixstowe** This attractive seaside resort is also Britain's largest container port. The town is renowned for its glorious gardens that run the length of the promenade. Along the seafront are the Spa Pavilion Theatre and a cinema. At Felixstowe Ferry, which is part of the old town, there is a ferry across the estuary to Bawdsey where there are several well-marked walks, popular with birdwatchers. At the other end of the town, on the Landguard Peninsula, is an observation quay where visitors can watch the ships going in and out of Felixstowe and Harwich, across the estuary in Essex. Landguard Fort, just behind the observation quay, was built by Henry VIII and is the only fort in England to have repelled an invasion attempt.

◀ **Clare** This small market town is situated between Melford and Haverhill on the north bank of the river Stour. It developed as a centre for the wool industry in the Middle Ages. This panoramic rooftop view of Clare can be seen from the castle mound situated in the country park two minutes' walk from the town centre. The mound has remnants of the old stone castle keep and close by are the old railway track and station – the only railway in the country ever to have been built inside castle grounds. The impressive roof and spire of the church of St Peter and St Paul are visible throughout the town. Many old houses in Clare are famous for their rough-cast decorative plasterwork called pargetting, applied to the outside walls.

27

RURAL ESSEX

The north of the county is famed for its pretty villages.

▶ **Finchingfield** This picture postcard village has a green, duckpond and a windmill, together with several medieval houses known as "cab-baches". Many of the cottages have decorative pargetting on their walls. The squat tower of the church of St John the Baptist stands at the top of Church Hill, looming behind the pretty 15th century dwelling which is home to the Causeway Tea Cottage.

▼ **Thaxted** Situated close to the river Chelmer, south of Saffron Walden, Thaxted is considered by many to be the jewel in the crown of Essex; it is full of interesting groups of buildings to charm the visitor. The town is dominated by the steeple of the cathedral-like church of St John. The alms-houses (below) are sited in the churchyard. Known as the Chantry, they were built as a priest's house.

▶ **Thaxted Morris** The town is the spiritual home of Morris dancing. The tradition was revived in 1911 by Mrs Miriam Noel, wife of the local vicar, Fr Conrad Noel. Today the Morris Men perform traditional Cotswold dances in Thaxted and its surrounding villages and towns between May and September. The annual gathering of Morris Men from all over England is an amazing spectacle. It takes place on the first weekend following the spring bank holiday and draws crowds from all over the country. The high point of the festival is the dancing of the Abbots Bromley Horn Dance late in the evening when the town is packed with visitors.

◀▶ Castle Hedingham The keep at Castle Hedingham is one of the best preserved in Europe. Aubrey de Vere, one of William the Conqueror's main supporters, built Castle Hedingham on land granted to him by William for his support during the invasion of England. The castle is surrounded by a beautiful deer park with a 15th century bridge which replaced the drawbridge and spans the now dry moat leading to the inner bailey. The park has an unusual dovecote and attractive lake. The village is a maze of narrow streets lined with pretty cottages, inns, restaurants and shops.

▲▼Ashdon The village of Ashdon lies on an ancient road within the rolling hills of the boulder clays of north-east Essex. It is surrounded by lush arable land and large areas of what was once a vast forest. Ashdon is steeped in history and has many interesting buildings. There were once 31 farms in the parish but today these have been

amalgamated into nine much larger farmsteads and many of the old farmhouses in or close to the village have been converted into homes. All Saints church at the top of Church Hill off Walden Road was rebuilt in stone in the early 11th century; originally it was a wooden structure. Ashdon is host to a kite festival which is held at Waltons Park each year in early June. The old railway carriage (above) is the only trace of a small station that was once on the edge of the village; part of the branch rail link which ran between Bartlow and Audley End, it was closed in May 1964. The Ashdon Village Collection, in Church Hill, is a museum of village life. Its fascinating displays cover agriculture, the home, shopping and entertainment.

CONSTABLE COUNTRY

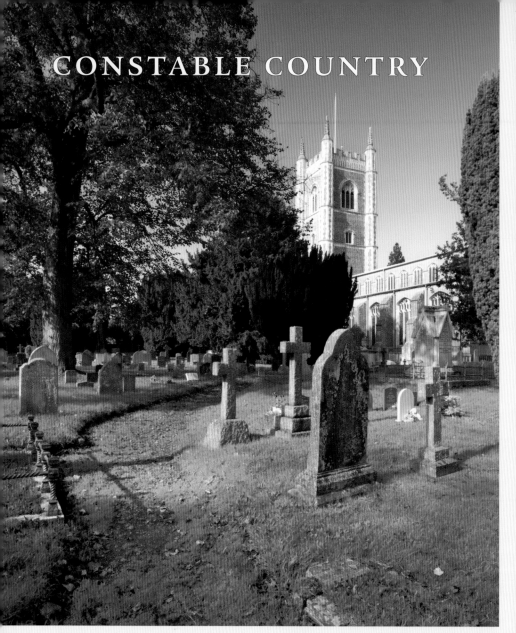

Dedham Vale, close to the river Stour between Suffolk and Essex, is known as Constable Country in memory of England's most famous landscape painter.

▲ **Dedham** The village of Dedham prospered as a wool town in the Middle Ages and many of its fine buildings date from this era. The parish church of St Mary the Virgin (above), constructed in 1492, was a favourite of John Constable and often features in his work. The church boasts one of the artist's few religious paintings, *The Ascension*, which hangs in the nave opposite the north porch.

▶ **Willy Lott's cottage** Just beyond Flatford Mill, this beautiful building is depicted in *The Hay Wain*, probably the most famous of all English landscape paintings.

▲◀ **Village scenes** Among the many fine buildings built during the wool boom in the village is the half-timbered Marlborough Head Hotel (above) in the town centre. Dedham Hall (far left) is the Old Grammar School where Constable studied; he walked here each day from his home at East Bergholt.

▶ **Church interior** As well as beautiful stained-glass windows, the interior of St Mary's church has some colourful shields mounted on the nave roof. These include depictions of *The Mayflower* which commemorate links with the town of Dedham Massachusetts where many local people emigrated, and the royal arms of Queen Elizabeth I. Dedham was at the centre of a fierce debate about the Sabbath among Puritans during her reign.

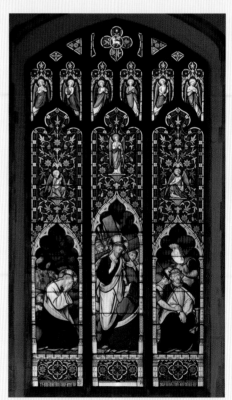

COLCHESTER

The capital of Roman Britain, Colchester is the oldest recorded town in Britain.

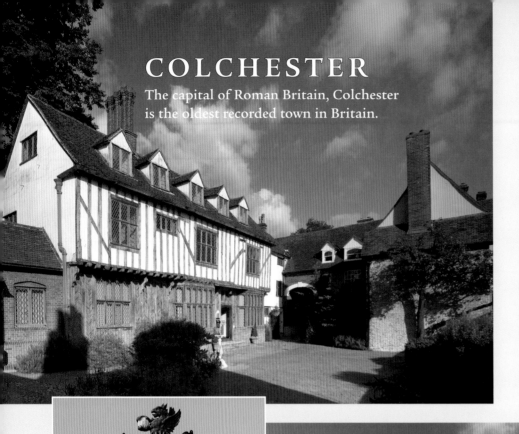

◄ **Clock Museum** Tymperleys Clock Museum is housed in a 15th century timber-framed building, once the home of William Gilberd, physician to Queen Elizabeth I. The beautiful clocks on display were made in Colchester, a centre of clock-making, between 1640-1860. The courtyard garden at Tymperleys is a welcome oasis of peace in the heart of the town.

▼ **The castle** Colchester Castle was constructed on the site of the Roman temple of Claudius by William the Conqueror in the same style as the White Tower in the Tower of London. Today it is an award-winning museum with many hands-on displays which illustrate Colchester's fascinating history from the Stone Age to the Civil War. The town hall, which dates from 1898-1902, is topped by the splendid 162ft Victoria Tower (below left).